Exploring Planets
EARTH

Susan Ring

WEIGL PUBLISHERS INC.

Published by Weigl Publishers Inc.
350 5th Avenue, Suite 3304, PMB 6G
New York, NY USA 10118-0069
Web site: www.weigl.com
Copyright 2004 WEIGL PUBLISHERS INC.

Library of Congress Cataloging-in-Publication Data

Ring, Susan.
  The earth / by Susan Ring.
     v. cm. -- (Exploring planets)
Includes index.
Contents: Introducing the earth -- What's in a name? -- Planet spotting
-- Early observations -- The earth in the solar system -- What's so
special about the earth? -- Missions to the earth -- Earth explorer:
John Glenn -- Earth explorer: Shannon Lucid -- The earth on the web --
Activity: earth physics: gravity -- What have you learned?
  ISBN 1-59036-104-0 (lib. bdg. : alk. paper) – ISBN 1-59036-231-4 (pbk.)
  1. Earth--Juvenile literature. [1. Earth.] I. Title. II. Series.
  QB631.4 .R58 2003
  525--dc21

                              2002014567

Printed in the United States of America
1 2 3 4 5 6 7 8 9 0 08 07 06 05 04

Photograph Credits

Every reasonable effort has been made to trace ownership and to obtain permission to reprint
copyright material. The publishers would be pleased to have any errors or omissions brought to their
attention so that they may be corrected in subsequent printings.

Cover: Digital Vision (top); Digital Vision (bottom)

Virginia Boulay: page 12; **COMSTOCK, Inc.:** page 8; **CORBIS/MAGMA:** page 6 (Gianni Dagli Orti);
Corel Corporation: page 10; **Digital Vision:** pages 11, 13, 14, 17; **NASA:** pages 1, 4, 7, 16, 18, 19, 22;
NASA JPL: page 9; **Bryan Pezzi:** page 21.

Project Coordinator Nicole Bezic King **Substantive Editor** Frances Purslow **Design** Terry Paulhus
Copy Editor Michelle Lomberg **Layout** Bryan Pezzi **Photo Researcher** Peggy Chan

Contents

Introducing Earth

Just like Mars or Jupiter, Earth is a planet. As humans work, play, and sleep, Earth is spinning on its **axis**. It is also **revolving** around the Sun. Have you ever thought about Earth as an object in space? The place that humans call home is a fascinating planet.

■ Earth moves very quickly. It spins on its axis at more than 1,000 miles (1,609 km) per hour.

Earth Facts

- Earth is more than 4.5 billion years old.

- Earth is the only planet with large amounts of liquid water on its surface.

- About three-quarters of Earth is covered with water. This is why it is sometimes called the "Blue Planet."

- Earth's **atmosphere** is made mostly of nitrogen and oxygen.

- Ice covers one-tenth of Earth's surface.

- The outer layer of Earth is called the **crust**. It is made of solid rock.

- Volcanoes are caused by hot liquid from inside Earth bursting through the crust.

Name That Planet

Many ancient peoples had **myths** about how Earth was formed. The Earth goddess had many names. The Romans called her *Tellus*. The Greeks called her *Gaea*. The name *Earth* comes from an Old English word.

The Maori of New Zealand called the sky *Rangi*. Earth was known as *Papa*. The Maori believed Rangi and Papa were in love. They were always hugging their children tightly between them. One of their children, the god of the forests, broke free. Rangi and Papa were separated, forming Earth and the sky.

■■ The Aztecs lived in what is now known as Mexico. Their name for the Earth goddess was *Coatlicue*.

Earth's Moon

Earth has only one moon. It is the fifth-largest moon in the **solar system**. In 1969, American astronauts visited the Moon. They walked on the surface. There is no wind or atmosphere on the Moon. This means the astronauts' footprints should stay on the surface forever.

From Earth, the Moon appears to change shape. These changes are called phases. Sometimes the Moon shines brightly. Other times it is not visible at all. The Moon does not make its own light. It **reflects** light from the Sun.

The Moon is the second-brightest object seen in the sky from Earth. The Sun is the brightest.

Planet Spotting

Sometimes the Moon's **orbit** causes it to pass directly between Earth and the Sun. When this happens, the Sun's light is blocked by the Moon. This event is called a solar eclipse. It is very dangerous to look directly at a solar eclipse. Even though the Sun is darkened, its rays can permanently damage the human eye.

■ The corona is the glowing area around the Sun. While it is part of the Sun's atmosphere, the corona is only visible during a solar eclipse.

See for Yourself

Imagine that you are in a spaceship orbiting Earth. What would you notice about the planet?

Photographs taken from space show many different features on Earth. Natural formations can be seen from space. These include the Grand Canyon, ice in Antarctica, and Earth's highest mountain, Mount Everest. Signs of human life, such as farms and cities, are also visible. Scientists can even watch dust storms and hurricanes as they develop.

■ This photo was taken from the space shuttle *Endeavour*. It is of Washington, D.C.

Early Observations

On a clear night, you can see many space objects from Earth. Planets and stars surround us. Throughout history, people have observed the sky. They have tried to understand Earth's position among the stars and planets.

The ancient Mayans thought that Earth was flat. They pictured the planet with four corners. Each corner of Earth was a different color. A jaguar at each corner held up the sky. The Mayans called these jaguars *bacabs*.

El Caracol is an ancient Mayan observatory.

Earth Watcher

Dr. Michael D. King heads NASA's Earth Observing System. He works with a team of scientists to study our planet.

The Earth Observing System uses **satellites** to study Earth. These satellites send data to Earth. Scientists use this information to learn more about Earth's land, atmosphere, water, and ice. Their observations help farmers, fishers, and **meteorologists**.

Meteorologists often use satellite images taken from space to predict the weather.

Earth in Our Solar System

Earth is one of the nine planets in our solar system. It is the third planet from the Sun.

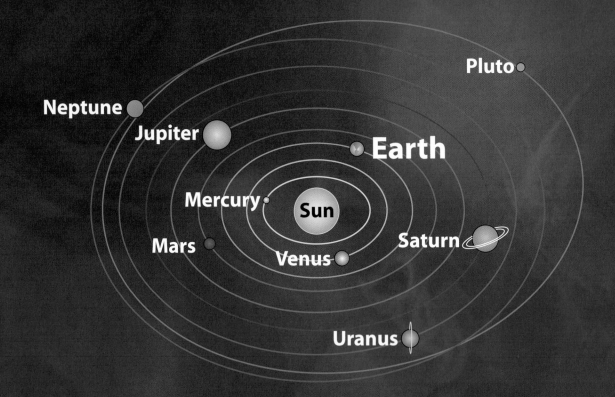

The oceans contain 97 percent of Earth's liquid water.

About 90 percent of Earth's ice covers Antarctica.

Comparing Earth

What makes Earth different from all of the other planets in our solar system? Earth has life on it.

Earth is the fifth-largest planet in the solar system. The largest planet is Jupiter. Jupiter's **radius** is more than eleven times larger than Earth's.

Earth is one of the rocky planets. Mercury, Venus, and Mars are also rocky planets. As the name suggests, these planets are made of rock.

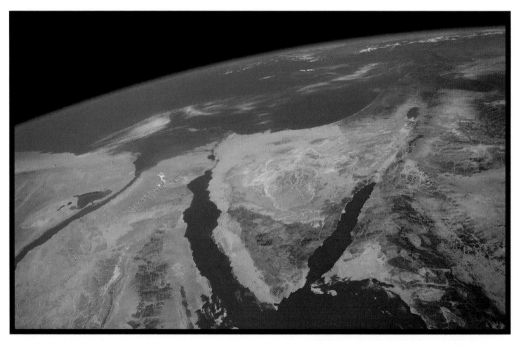

Earth's water supports life on land and under water. This makes our planet unique in our solar system.

Compare the Planets

	PLANET FEATURES				
PLANET	**Distance from the Sun**	**Days to Orbit the Sun**	**Diameter**	**Length of Day**	**Average Temperature**
Mercury	36 million miles (58 million km)	88	3,032 miles (4,880 km)	4,223 hours	333° Fahrenheit (167° C)
Venus	67 million miles (108 million km)	225	7,521 miles (12,104 km)	2,802 hours	867° Fahrenheit (464° C)
Earth	93 million miles (150 million km)	365	7,926 miles (12,756 km)	24 hours	59° Fahrenheit (15° C)
Mars	142 million miles (229 million km)	687	4,222 miles (6,975 km)	25 hours	−81° Fahrenheit (−63° C)
Jupiter	484 million miles (779 million km)	4,331	88,846 miles (142,984 km)	10 hours	−230° Fahrenheit (−146° C)
Saturn	891million miles (1,434 million km)	10,747	74,897 miles (120,535 km)	11 hours	−285° Fahrenheit (−176° C)
Uranus	1,785 million miles (2,873 million km)	30,589	31,763 miles (51,118 km)	17 hours	−355° Fahrenheit (−215° C)
Neptune	2,793 million miles (4,495 million km)	59,800	30,775 miles (49,528 km)	16 hours	−355° Fahrenheit (−215° C)
Pluto	3,647 million miles (5,869 million km)	90,588	1,485 miles (2,390)	153 hours	−375° Fahrenheit (−226° C)

Missions from Earth

Satellites and other spacecraft help scientists study Earth. To explore the solar system, scientists use **space probes**. Space probes have taken photographs and mapped planet surfaces. They have collected valuable information for scientific study. Pluto is the only planet in our solar system that has not been visited by a space probe.

People are now living and working in space. Astronauts from many countries are aboard the *International Space Station*. They are learning more about life in space and the effect of **gravity**.

■ The first astronauts to visit the *International Space Station* stayed there for 4 months.

Life on Earth

Why is there life on Earth? Earth has special features that allow living things to survive. Two main features are Earth's atmosphere and water.

Earth's atmosphere protects Earth from the Sun's harmful rays. The atmosphere is made up mostly of two gases: nitrogen and oxygen. Plants and animals need these gases to survive.

Water is also necessary for life. Without water, no living thing could survive.

■ Earth's atmosphere looks like a thin blue layer when viewed from space.

Planet People

John Glenn

John Glenn is a legend in Earth exploration. He was the first American to orbit Earth. In 1962, he launched into space aboard a rocket. It took 5 hours for John to travel around Earth 3 times.

In 1998, John made history again. At age 77, he journeyed for a second time into space.

■ Twelve years after his first voyage into space, John Glenn became an American senator.

Shannon Lucid

Name: Shannon Lucid
Earth Accomplishments:
Has spent the most hours in orbit of any woman

Shannon Lucid works for NASA. As NASA's Chief Scientist, she leads a team that will shape future space exploration. Shannon holds the record for having the most hours in orbit of any woman in the world. She recently spent 223 days in space on board the Russian space station *Mir*. She is the first woman to receive the U.S. Congressional Space Medal of Honor.

Shannon Lucid has made a total of five voyages into space.

Earth on the Internet

To learn more about Earth, look for books at your school library. The Internet is also an excellent place to learn about Earth. There are many great Web sites with information. Just type the words *Earth* and *planet* into a search engine. Google and Yahoo are useful search engines.

The Internet has information on all of the planets in our solar system. To learn about the nine planets, visit these Web sites:

Encarta Homepage
www.encarta.com
Type the name of a planet that you would like to learn about into the search engine.

NASA Kids
http://kids.msfc.nasa.gov
NASA built a Web site for young learners just like you. Visit this site to learn more about the nine planets, space travel, and the latest NASA news.

Young Scientists at Work

Earth's Gravity

Gravity is a very strong force. It keeps people from floating off the surface of Earth into space. Gravity also keeps Earth orbiting around the Sun. What would happen if there was no gravity?

Attach a piece of string to a small rubber ball. Then, go outside. Hold the end of the string in your hand. Begin to swing the ball around in a circle. The ball represents Earth, and your hand is the Sun. The string is the gravity that keeps Earth orbiting around the Sun. While you are swinging the ball, let go of the string. What happens? This is what would happen if there were no gravity.

What Have You Learned?

How much do you know about Earth?
Test your knowledge!

1 What happens when the Moon passes between Earth and the Sun?

2 How fast are the winds on the Moon?

3 True or False? Earth's atmosphere is made mostly of nitrogen and oxygen.

4 What is the name of Earth's highest mountain?

5 Who was the first American astronaut to orbit Earth?

6 On Earth, how many days equal 1 year?

7 Why is Earth sometimes called the Blue Planet?

8 True or False? Earth is the third planet from the Sun.

9 What makes the Moon shine brightly?

10 What are some things that weather satellites can photograph from space?

What was your score?

9–10	You should work at NASA!
5–8	Not too bad for an earthling!
0–4	You need to polish your telescope!

Answers

1 A solar eclipse **2** There is no wind on the Moon. **3** True **4** Mount Everest is the highest mountain on Earth. **5** John Glenn was the first American astronaut to orbit Earth. **6** On Earth, 1 year equals 365 days. **7** Earth is called the Blue Planet because about three-quarters of it is covered in water. **8** True **9** The Moon reflects light from the Sun. **10** Weather satellites can photograph storms and hurricanes

Words to Know

atmosphere: the layer of gases surrounding a planet

axis: an imaginary line on which a planet spins

crust: the top layer of a rocky planet or moon

gravity: a force that pulls things toward the center

meteorologists: scientists who study the weather

myths: stories or legends, often about gods or heroes

orbit: the nearly circular path a space object makes around another object in space

radius: a straight line that extends from the center of a circle to its edge

reflects: gives back light

revolving: moving around in a circle

satellites: space objects that orbit another space object

solar system: the Sun, the planets, and other objects that move around the Sun

space probes: spacecraft used to gather information about space

Index